The Formula for a
Rich Life

5 Steps to Earning More, Working
Less & Building a Quality of Life

Dawn Connelly

ISBN: 978-0-9975425-1-6

Lifting Up Leaders, LLC,
100 SW Albany Ave,
Stuart, FL 34994
DawnConnelly.com

The Formula for a
Rich Life

5 Steps to Earning More, Working Less & Building a Quality of Life

Dawn Connelly

This book is dedicated to my amazing husband Brian who has stood by my side and believed in me since middle school! Thank you for your love, support, encouragement and prayers!

Testimonials

"Just 30 minutes a week with a dynamic leadership coach like Dawn Connelly drives our Think Tank members to excel in our industry and to build exceptional businesses."

— Patricia Vice, CRM, FAI,
Owner of Texas Security Shredding

"Dare I say that I consider meeting Dawn a 'God-thing.' I have been banging my head against the ceiling trying to take my business to the next level. Dawn's leadership skills training, Think Tank coaching, helpful practices, curriculum and accountability will no doubt be the final force I need to break through."

— Susan Dawson Whittington, CRPC®,
Financial Advisor, Financial Planning
Associate & Portfolio Manager for Espinal,
Stern & Whittington at Morgan
Stanley Wealth Management

"Dawn hit it out of the park with every principle that she unveiled at her workshop and Think Tank. Each person, including me, received a new level of success in their dreams, goals and relationships. I can't say enough about the breakthrough that I experienced!"

— Lynne Barletta,
Founder and Executive Director of
Visionary School of Arts and
Visionary Centers International

"I stand in awe of Dawn's honesty, determination, courage, and...the majesty of her commitment to improving lives through leadership, and being a pillar of influence. I also stand in awe of her well known voice as a speaker, teacher, coach and author."

— Rick Ruperto, PhD,
Director of Business Development,
2TouchPOS

"Caution! Dawn Connelly is serious about the powerful impact that leadership training and focused mentoring has. *Formula for a Rich Life* will motivate, stimulate and enrich readers with fresh ideas laid out in an interesting, informative, hands-on approach."

— Sam Bicking,
Owner of Docu-Shred, LLC

"It's important to choose business trainers who have already accomplished what they teach. Dawn Connelly is a shining example of this. She has an incredible giving spirit. Who better to learn from than someone who has been successful in business and in life!"

— Caroline Barca,
Real Estate Agent

"Dawn's passion for others is palpable. When you're working with her on any project, you know she's laser-focused on helping you achieve maximum impact. You walk away feeling inspired, refreshed and ready to roll. She's a true powerhouse!"

— Karen Vaughn,
President & Founder of Raising World Changers

"Whether she's at a casual dinner, with business associates or giving the keynote at an industry conference, Dawn has a genuine interest in the lives of the individuals around her. She truly cares about your success in both business and life."

— Karen Metz, CITRMS,
Owner & President of Keystone Mobile Shredding, Inc.

"Dawn inspires and challenges me to stretch and grow. After spending time with her, I leave refreshed, buzzing with ideas and excited about life. Everyone should have a mentor or trainer like this in their life!"

— Katie Schwaderer,
Accenture Marketing and Social Media Specialist

"My life is definitely richer for knowing Dawn. Richer relationally, richer spiritually and richer materially. I believe that poverty, the opposite of being rich, isn't about money, but rather about broken and distorted relationships. Dawn's insights on life, purpose, business and relationships are contagious and all point to one outcome...richness."

— D. Bart Justice,
President, Secure Destruction Service
& Chairman, GraceLink International

"Dawn is part of my-nothing-is-impossible community. She inspires me to do my best thinking. Her work will make a heartfelt impact on your life."

— Wendy McDonell,
Founder and CEO of Heart to Mind Leadership Inc.

"In a world filled with marketing and sound bites, Dawn has ideas that will help you in your everyday life, from overcoming struggles you face to having the successful and fulfilled life you are striving for."

— Stephen Owens,
Entrepreneur & Business Owner

"Dawn Connelly is one of the most passionate and helpful people I have ever met. A master at connecting with people from the inside-out, she truly understands human nature on a very deep level. As such, she has a rare ability to get to the core of an issue with solutions. I am grateful that our paths have crossed for I am a much better person because of Dawn."

— Patti Kadkhodaian,
President AJAKO Promotional Products

"Dawn is a natural born communicator, coach and leader. Her positivity and daily outlook transcends anything negative you may have going on in your life. She is one of the most genuine people I know, and I am so privileged to have her be a part of my life. I am proud to consider her a great friend."

— Don Gerard, Jr., CPA, CSDS,
Head Shredder Dude, Landshark Shredding

"No one can truly impact a complex family life and business if they do not have a rich, healthy inner self. Dawn has navigated complex demands for many years, and now she shares her best kept secrets! What she shares is real life. What she offers is real freedom with her 5 simple steps. These are lessons that will leave a legacy of fulfillment!"

— Sue Matrunola,
Bible Teacher, International Life Coach,
and Inspirational Speaker

"During the course of my work day, I have successfully applied Dawn's teachings to areas that I have previously struggled with, which has enabled me to enjoy my work more, and spend less time at work and more time at home. Besides helping me professionally, Dawn has also helped my personal and spiritual growth."

— Elizabeth Carrillo,
Office Manager at Porcaro Cosmetic Surgery

"Dawn has helped me achieve goals for myself and has held me accountable to those goals. As a result, we're able to increase the success of our team. Dawn is a great and insightful listener. I would recommend Dawn to anyone who is committed to improving their leadership skills, personal growth and their company's bottom line."

— Steve Watters,
Retail Market Manager - Treasure Coast,
Harbor Community Bank

The Formula for a Rich Life

INTRODUCTION

Live a Rich Life!

Did you think things would be different for you at this point in your life? Did you imagine you'd be wealthier, happier or less stressed? Are you tired of feeling over-worked and overwhelmed? Are you tired of not having enough time to devote to yourself and your loved ones? Are you tired of wishing you earned more money? Are you tired of wishing you'd built more wealth? Or that you just had more time to enjoy the wealth you've created?

This is your chance to stop being tired and start being transformed.

Maybe you love what you do. Or perhaps you consider your work to be "just a job." Either way, I wrote this book to help you live a bigger and better life. As you read, you'll discover how to boost your income, build your business, enjoy more free time and improve the quality of your relationships.

This is your chance to live with purpose and joy. Because you deserve to live a life that matters. A life that fulfills you. A life with no regrets.

I wish I could tell you that I've lived a regret-free life. But that's not where my journey began. My road to a regret-free life began many years ago. At the age of 25, my husband and I were earning over half-a-million dollars per year. We had just built our million dollar dream home in Chicago. We were members of the exclusive East Bank Club, working out with Oprah Winfrey, Barack Obama and Michael Jordan. We were rich, but there was a problem: We were living a poor life.

I had no quality of life. I spent very little time with my family. I worked all the time. I was rich on paper, but in my life, I was anything but rich.

And I wanted a rich life.

I had to make a change. After 9 years as a trial lawyer for a top international law firm, I left corporate America to build a business as a real estate investor. In just a few short years, I successfully flipped 12 homes in South Florida and was featured in Money Magazine for my foreclosure investing. In that time, I also built an international team in a direct sales company, where I was promoted to Regional Vice President in record-setting time. And then, a few years later, I joined the #1 leadership guru in the world and became a certified John Maxwell coach. Since then, I've trained thousands of people in personal and professional development.

With time and intention, I created a life that felt rich and fulfilling.

But this is when things took another turn. I was happy as a working mom. Until I wasn't. Suddenly, I felt a tug. Something still wasn't quite right. So, I shocked my friends and family (but perhaps myself most of all) by deciding to become a full-time stay-at-home mom when my husband and I had our fourth child. Surprisingly, those were the hardest two years of my journey. But those years changed everything. That's when I learned to live a truly Rich Life.

When I decided to go back to work two years later, I chose to only do work that I loved. I was earning over $10,000 per month. Finally, I had discovered the formula for a Rich Life. I learned how to spend time doing only the things that I do best. That's when I began earning over $5,000 for just one hour of time. That number continues to grow. I am a focused and intentional mother and wife.

I have time for hobbies, fitness, vacations and cooking. I've grown my income, and my life is rich.

Today, I am so excited to share with you the formula for living a Rich Life. I've developed this formula based on my life experience—both the big wins and the devastating mistakes. I hope my story will inspire you to evaluate your life so that you can live a Rich Life, too. My message comes from my heart—from the place where I discovered the truth of what it means to live a fulfilling, meaningful and purposeful life.

My hope for this book is that you stop living with the fear of regret, stop stressing out about all the things on your plate, stop feeling guilty for the time you are not spending with your loved ones and stop worrying about money.

Today is a big day. It can be the day you learn to live the way you have always dreamed about. You are about to discover five powerful—yet simple—steps to increase your income, boost your sales and build your business, all while improving the quality of your life. I'm so excited to share what I have learned about how to make money and love your life at the same time. Thank you for having the courage and desire to live a Rich Life. You are going to love this journey!

The Formula for a Rich Life

I'm thrilled to share with you the incredible, powerful and simple formula to increase sales, grow your income, create more quality free time and live a no-regret life!

With the tools I give you, you'll also learn:

- the simple strategy to earn more money while working less

- how to select and surround yourself with people who can help you live a prosperous and Rich Life

- how to boost your business by being a person people *have to* work with

- how to have incredibly fulfilling relationships and lead a truly Rich Life

- and much, much more!

THE RICH LIFE ON THE FLY!

My decision to cultivate a Rich Life began with quite an epiphany.

It happened a few years ago while my husband, Brian, and I were on vacation in Orlando with our three kids. I had gotten up early one morning to take a walk around the lake at the resort property. During that walk, I began thinking about all that was going on in my life. You see, I was pregnant with our fourth child. I was also working tirelessly to move up to the next level in my business. I had achieved record-breaking success and had even become somewhat of a minor celebrity in my professional circles. It was a time of excitement but also great stress. In fact, I distinctly remember asking myself:

"How many people today actually have four children?"

"Are we crazy?"

"How am I going to balance all this?"

And then, "How can I find a nanny who can care for our kids and our new baby so that I can continue to lead my team to the very top?"

As soon as I asked myself that last question, I heard the audible voice of God for the first time in my life. It said:

"You don't need a nanny, you're the mom."

I could barely comprehend what I'd heard.

Never in a million years would I have considered leaving behind my professional life and the independence I'd enjoyed from having my own career. And yet in that moment, I knew I was called to do just that. I was scared, but I knew that if I didn't make this decision, I would be filled with regret. I knew that I had no choice but to walk away from it all. And I would be walking toward a life that I thought was for other women, but not for me: being a stay-at-home mom.

The next two years were the most humbling of my life. In a single day, I left a high six-figure income and a prestigious position. People started to question my dedication and emotional stability. I was, after all, four months pregnant with baby number four! But I stuck with my decision, and over the next two years I stayed home to raise our four children. While on that journey, I discovered the formula for living a Rich Life.

That discovery is the heart and soul of this book, and I am so excited to share it with you! These proven strategies and tools can help you increase your income, build your business and enhance your quality of life, just like they did for me.

This book is dedicated to helping you discover the sheer bliss that comes when you learn how to maximize your results and your happiness on the climb to success.

Life on the Fly

Living a Rich Life also means learning to do what I call "Living on the Fly."

The idea for a Life on the Fly came to me one day as I was watching my husband take down our Christmas lights. He was up on a ladder that he had propped up against our house. It was one of those extendable ladders—you know, the kind where a section slides up to help you reach even higher? He'd needed to reach our roof to take down the lights,

so he had extended the sliding section of the ladder up toward the sky.

In that moment, I didn't just see a ladder. I also saw something deeper. Something more meaningful.

Our lives are just like that ladder. It can seem that we only have a limited reach. Like, maybe this is all there is? But, if you are reading this book, it's because you believe there must be more. And there is!

Did you know that the extendable part of the ladder is literally called the "fly?" It is. And like that ladder, we all have the ability to be extended. I want to share with you the exact formula to harness your potential and Live on the Fly. Life on the Fly means becoming more productive and more prosperous. It means enjoying our careers and our relationships. It is the key to building wealth—the kind of wealth that makes life worth living. Wealth not only in money, but in your quality of life.

And this is where a Rich Life and a Life on the Fly come together. Living a Rich Life is really about pulling up and out the very best part of you. Those who live a Rich Life also enjoy Life on the Fly. Extending our own fly—our own soaring potential—can help us to reach our highest heights.

The fly stretches us, maximizes us and brings us closer to our destination: our ideal life, and our Rich Life.

And best of all? Living on the Fly is exhilarating. It transforms us. It frees us from regret. And it gives us a number of gifts and benefits, including:

- Increased income and sales
- More free time
- Increased productivity and efficiency
- Fulfilling relationships
- Clarity of purpose
- Peace
- Self-awareness to be the very best version of you
- A core group of thinking partners and advisers
- Deeper connections to people
- Goal realization
- A legacy

This book will teach you how to achieve these goals. It will teach you how to maximize your time, become supernaturally efficient and increase your bottom line. You'll discover exactly how to spend your time in a way that increases your income, your results, your success and your significance.

Are you ready to learn how to stretch yourself so that you can reach previously unreachable heights? Are you ready to discover how you can work less but earn more? Are you ready to make space for more quality free time to build meaningful relationships? I hope so. I want you to discover the regret-free life I have learned to live.

I want you to learn how to Live on the Fly.

For we can achieve our greatest human potential—and we can lead a truly Rich Life—when we Live on the Fly.

STEP ONE:
MANAGE EXPECTATIONS

Imagine having more time every day to be able to focus on key income-building activities. What if I could teach you how to use this time so that you could yield the greatest financial return on your time investment? What if I could also teach you how to gain spare time to improve your personal life?

I'm about to show you how to gain that time. I will show you a tool that can literally shave hours of time off your day. And I will give you the formula for how to use this new free time to build your income and improve your relationships with your loved ones.

What Are YOUR Expectations?

I work with a lot of entrepreneurs and professionals who come to me to help them get better results. Most of the time, they want to take their business to the next level. They want help generating more leads, more sales and more revenue. I love to help them with that. And I'm good at it. But, as an executive coach, mother and wife, I can't do that effectively without looking at the whole picture of their life.

You see, a Rich Life does not come from money alone. A Rich Life means building deep relationships and having time for things we love doing. It means prioritizing ourselves and our loved ones and acting according to our priorities.

The two things I am the most proud of today are my marriage and my children. But there was a time when the thing I was the most proud of was my career. And during that time, I was living with regret and guilt about the time I wasn't spending with my husband and children.

I needed to make some changes in my priorities and my expectations in order to live a truly Rich Life.

Do you know your priorities? Have you taken time to list them in numerical order? There is no right or wrong order — only one that is right for your life. Where does your spouse or significant other fit in? Your children? Grandchildren? What about you — your health, spiritual time and hobbies? I can tell you that relationships can bring the greatest joy but also the deepest pain in our lives. But this potential pain shouldn't prevent us from prioritizing our relationships. Both the joy and the pain give us meaning—they give our lives meaning. In fact, when you prioritize your relationships properly and act accordingly, your life will immediately become richer.

In our workshops, I teach specific strategies you can use to better prioritize your loved ones so that you can begin to experience the richness of quality relationships. But right now, I'd like to show you some key principles to help you find more time for yourself and your loved ones.

Manage Others' Expectations

Living a Rich Life requires you to start managing expectations. It's one of the greatest pitfalls I see when I work with my clients. It's also one of the easiest things to fix.

A great way to begin to manage expectations is to value your own time. By valuing your own time and letting your clients, patients, staff and others know that you have boundaries and expectations, they too will respect your time.

When I used to practice law in Chicago, I worked at a top international law firm. There were over 300 lawyers in my office. One of those lawyers was a man named Jeff. Jeff is a very smart attorney. He is likeable and funny. He's a good friend of mine, too. But he is a prime example of what happens when you fail to respect your own time and set expectations.

I used to arrive at the office by 7:30 a.m. This time was sacred to me. The office was usually quiet, and I could work for at least an hour without distraction. Jeff, however, would usually roll in between 8:30 and 9:00 a.m. By that point, the hustle and bustle of the office had already begun. Yet rather than starting his billable day, Jeff would grab a coffee and make his rounds. He would stop at just about every associate's door to say hello.

The partners took notice. Jeff would often get a huge assignment at 5:30 p.m. Why? Well, because if Jeff didn't value his own time, why should the firm's partners value it?

On the other hand, I would go in early, work efficiently, and leave as close to 6 o'clock as possible. This wasn't just a professional decision: it was also a personal decision. My husband was trading options at the time, and the bell at the Board of Options Exchange rang at 3 o'clock. I knew that every hour I was up in my office after 3 o'clock was an hour I was missing with him and our infant daughter.

The simple act of respecting my own time caused the partners to respect it, too. I'm not saying there weren't times when I was brought in on an emergency project, but the majority of the time, they respected the boundaries I set. And I didn't simply set those boundaries with my words: I set them with my actions. On the other hand, Jeff's disregard for his time caused those he worked for to be less respectful of his time. They expected that he would be available late into the evening, so he became the go-to associate for late night projects.

> Let your actions speak for you. When you show people that you value your time—both your professional time and your personal time—they will come to value it, too.

Think about your own actions and expectations for a moment: Are you acting in a way that lets others know you respect your time? What boundaries are you setting? Do you make your health a priority? Do you make your family a priority?

Let your actions speak for you. When you show people that you value your time—both your professional time and your personal time—they will come to value it, too.

How to Successfully Manage Expectations

What message are you sending? Here are a few simple, life-changing steps you can take to begin to set boundaries and expectations.

1. Set the Expectation Up Front – You can really set yourself up for success simply by letting your client, boss or whomever know your time limitations before you begin talking or meeting with them. For example, if you call a client to respond to a question, you can start by saying, "Hello Sue, it's Dawn. I wanted to get back to you. I only have 15 minutes before my next appointment, but I wanted to make sure I addressed your concern as soon as possible."

2. Set an Autoresponder – You don't have to check every single e-mail the second it hits your inbox. Instead, you can set an autoresponder so that when you receive an e-mail, an automatic message goes to the sender saying something like, "Thank you for your message. It is very important to me. I check my e-mails twice a day, at 10:00 a.m. and 4:00 p.m. I will respond to your message at that time. If this is an emergency, you can call my assistant at…" Another good option is to ask the person to text you if you do not have an assistant. Most cell phones allow you to send similar auto-response messages, too.

3. <u>Set Limits On After-Hours Availability</u> – Consider letting your clients, patients, boss and staff know that after 6:00 p.m., you are not available except for emergencies. You can even consider making yourself available during your lunch hour or one night a week after 6:00 p.m. if you'd like to be more available to meet your clients' needs. You will find they will value and respect your time more. Furthermore, the sheer act of having to wait to call you will eliminate those impulsive emergencies that, with time, are often not all that urgent or important.

4. <u>Set Problem-Solving Hours</u> – A great way to gain back time and to empower your team is to set a specific time of the day that you "problem-solve." For example, let your team know that they can come to you with their questions, concerns, issues and problems at 3 o'clock. Not only will you be able to devote a set time to solving their problems, you'll reduce the number of interruptions and teach your team to be more independent. If they have to wait until 3 o'clock to come to you, they are much more likely to find an answer on their own and develop their own problem-solving skills.

Do Tasks One at a Time

Research shows that when we interrupt our current task to do something else—whether it's answering the phone, responding to an e-mail, answering a question from a co-worker or employee or completing some other activity—it takes us a full 11 minutes to get back to the place where we were before the interruption. That means if you are interrupted just four times a day, you are losing almost 45 minutes each day! You could literally gain back over three-and-a-half hours a week by choosing to focus on one activity at a time and managing expectations.

Managing your team's and your clients' expectations can dramatically increase your efficiency. Follow number 4 above, and let them know your problem-solving hour of the day. This simple modification can help you gain back hours each week—not only for you, but also for your team. They will learn to continue working and problem-solving on their own rather than interrupting their task to come interrupt you for an answer.

You can also try consolidating tasks that tend to be spread out over the course of the day. For instance, as I showed you in my example above, stop responding to e-mails as they come in. Instead, select one or two specific times throughout the day to respond. If you have set the expectation that you do not respond immediately to texts and e-mails, people stop expecting it. Moreover, your productivity and efficiency will soar.

Manage Technology

We are living in a time where people expect they should be able to reach us at any given time. That is not an expectation you should succumb to. It comes at a cost. I can almost hear some of you saying, "But Dawn, if I don't take my client's 7:00 p.m. call, the client will find another realtor, mortgage broker, lawyer, [fill in the blank]." They might, but they probably won't. If you have built your business with your communication skills—which I address in Step Four—your clients will be willing to wait for you. It really comes down to managing their expectations.

An important motto I teach my clients to live by is that their urgency is not your emergency. But it will feel like an emergency if you are always taking their calls at all hours of the day and night. So imagine, for a moment, the worst thing that could happen if you changed this behavior. If you don't take the call in the evenings and someone has to leave a voicemail, is that so bad? What if you text them a response that you are busy with a family commitment, but you will call them first thing in the morning? Will they hire someone else? Will anything really change if you get back to them in the morning? Stop giving in to their microwave mentality. It doesn't have to be RIGHT NOW.

When I was working in my direct sales business, I had an international team. I was leading thousands of people who depended on me for their success, training and growth. I made the mistake of living at my team's beck and call. I provided the very best service, but it came at a price to my family. My cell phone was like an appendage of my body. I felt naked when I didn't have it on me. My children became accustomed to me talking to them while I was responding to an "ever so important" text. But you know what? My team didn't respect my time because I didn't respect my time. And my family life was suffering.

Can you relate?

Several months later, I decided to implement a policy that changed everything. I let everyone on my team and all my customers know that from 5:00 to 8:00 p.m., I was unavailable. I explained this was my family time: It was the time when my kids needed me. Thus, during this time, I charged my cell phone in my bedroom and turned the ringer off.

I can't express to you the peace this brought to me and to my family. My kids were ecstatic.

It's amazing how different a conversation is when you are actually looking the person in the eyes and listening to them. My children's behavior and the quality of our relationships reflected this truth. And you know what? Nothing awful ever happened as a result of me being unavailable during that time. In fact, it taught my team that they, too, needed to respect their own time.

What valuable lessons can you, your colleagues, your clients or your family learn about managing expectations? You might be surprised by just how much richness these lessons add to your life.

What Message Are You Sending?

What can you do to set boundaries? How can you begin to live out your priorities better? Do your past behaviors reflect your current priorities? To answer these questions, I often ask my clients to look at their credit card and bank statements. By assessing your past credit card and bank statements along with your calendar entries for the past 1, 3 or 6 months, you'll gain tremendous insight on how you can change your life to honor your priorities better.

For example, let's say that your top priorities are spending more quality time with your spouse and getting back in shape. What have you done in the past 60 days to honor these priorities? If you look back at your calendar, how many date nights are on there? How many weekend getaways have you taken together? How often is exercise in your daily agenda?

What about your bank account? Where are you spending your money? Is it on creating special memories with your spouse? Or even on marriage counseling, if that is what you need? Is there a gym membership on there? Are you using it? Is the food you are buying healthy? How often are you eating out?

I coached a top real estate agent who used to get text messages at all hours of the day and night. For those of you in real estate, you can probably relate: There are some clients for whom everything is an "emergency." But this particular real estate agent and her team adopted a great tactic. They set an autoresponder for when they were driving that sent the following text: "My team and I took the challenge not to text and drive. I will respond to your text when I arrive safely at my destination." She got more compliments than you can imagine just by using that simple strategy. And she didn't lose a single client.

Are you beginning to see all the ways you can manage expectations? At my workshops, we explore even more strategies and creative solutions to teach you how to free your time, focus on your priorities and truly Live on the Fly. Now, I'd like to show you how to use what I call your "Inner Table" to help you strategize some of these best practices.

STEP ONE:
MANAGE EXPECTATIONS
ACTION QUESTIONS

"A little knowledge that acts is worth infinitely more than much knowledge that is idle."

— Kahlil Gibran

1. Do your expectations (or lack thereof) ever lead to negative results? What specific negative results do you notice?

_____

_____

_____

_____

2. What limitations have you set on your availability with your team?

_____

_____

_____

_____

3. What limitations have you set on your availability with your clients, customers or patients?

_____

_____

_____

_____

_____

4. How have you communicated your limitations to your team, clients, customers or patients?

_____

_____

_____

_____

_____

5. What are your biggest challenges when it comes to the clarity of your expectations?

_____

_____

_____

_____

_____

6. How can you revise these expectations to get the results you are looking for?

_____

_____

_____

_____

_____

_____

_____

7. Do these revised expectations reflect your priorities?

_____

_____

_____

_____

_____

_____

_____

STEP TWO:
BUILD YOUR INNER TABLE

The Blueprint for a Rich Life on the Fly

I'm about to show you the blueprint to building your team for success! Have you ever heard the saying that your income is a direct result of the five people you hang around most? This is your chance to hand pick people who will come alongside you as you build your Rich Life. They are the ones who make it possible for you to extend your fly. They will stretch you and encourage you.

It's time to build your A-team. I'm going to teach you how to assemble your Inner Table and how to use them to design your Rich Life. Your Inner Table is an essential part of building your Life on the Fly. This team will challenge you, problem-solve with you and believe in you, even when you don't believe in yourself. They are the magic behind you.

The Role of an Inner Table

Marcia is a client of mine who worked for years for a big insurance company. This past year, she finally made the decision to leave and start her own insurance company. As you might imagine, this was a huge step for her. She was starting pretty much from scratch with her client base. Marcia knew she needed to surround herself with people who could guide her and keep her focused on the most important tasks in front of her—people who could help her build her business and her income the fastest.

Marcia joined one of my Think Tanks. A Think Tank is a group that is part-brainstorming and part-coaching. It is a place where people can collaborate and share ideas, challenges and solutions with one another. What Marcia didn't realize is that this Think Tank would end up functioning as her Inner Table. The members of the Think Tank helped her to discover the highest impact activities to build her business. They held her accountable and helped her to solve problems.

Marcia was a solo-preneur. She did not have an assistant, let alone a staff. But she knew she had the potential to take her company and build something substantial. And she knew better than to do it alone. She needed our help. After a few short weeks, Marcia had armed herself with practices and strategies to build a very successful insurance business.

Then Marcia came to my workshop where she learned to get more done in less time. She discovered skills to build her business with referrals. She mastered how to focus on the activities that generated the most business and income. She built a huge referral business.

After just one year of venturing off on her own, Marcia has more business than she ever imagined. She was able to bring on an assistant. Her income grew to over $10,000 a month with the skills she developed from my Think Tank and workshop.

Do you want to know the secret to this kind of success? Develop an Inner Table. That's where the magic happens.

Assemble Your Inner Table

Your Inner Table is a small, intimate and influential group of people whom you can rely on and trust. They share common goals and interests with you. They are your thinking partners and mentors. They will provide you with the greatest growth, thinking and accountability.

Your Inner Table will help you create a clear vision, problem-solve and stay accountable to your priorities. The people in your Inner Table serve as your launching pad and sounding board. And you need them to build the life you are seeking!

When you are selecting the members for your Inner Table, give it a lot of thought. It's important that you choose your members wisely. Your Inner Table can make you...or break you. Be intentional. Be deliberate. Strive for people who are loyal and faithful, and who have wisdom, integrity and specialized knowledge.

Who Has a Seat at Your Inner Table?

My own greatest ideas and accomplishments have come from intentional, purposeful relationships. Your Inner Table is your chance to cultivate these relationships. You don't have to study uber-successful people just yet—you'll learn more about this in Step Five. For now, simply focus on inviting four to six key people to your Inner Table.

Following is an image of your Inner Table. All you need to do is write your name in at the head of the table. Around the table, you'll see five additional chairs. Consider placing your spouse or significant other, if you have one, at the other head of the table. In this case, there will be four chairs remaining. Fill them carefully.

Once you have made your "guest list," start inviting them. I like to invite them to coffee or lunch, where I explain I am assembling my core team—my Inner Table. I tell them how much I admire them and value their feedback in my life. I invite them to be a part of my Inner Table and explain that we can learn from each other and help stretch one another to achieve our goals.

In your own conversations, make sure your "guests" know that being a part of your Inner Table is not a huge time commitment: maybe only 30-60 minutes a month. But let them know, too, that this short time will deliver powerful results for both of you.

Decide on the frequency of your meetings. You should meet at least monthly. Furthermore, your meetings can be virtual or in person.

In our workshops, we discuss how to select and invite to your Inner Table and how to use them to accomplish all your goals in greater detail. If this process is done correctly, you will see huge results with minimal effort and time investment.

What is Your Role at Your Inner Table?

No one ever rises above the need for good counsel and wisdom. We all need an Inner Table in all seasons of life. Be teachable. Be coachable. If you make it hard for people to coach you, they won't. So make it easy for them to speak into your life.

When I was leading my direct sales team, I taught every new team member my system. It worked. It was proven and tested. I would tell them to follow the system to a "T" for the first few months. Then, they could modify it and adjust it.

Every once in a while, someone would join my team and refuse to be coachable. I remember one man who had just joined my team and who was incredibly successful in the business world. He had hundreds of employees and had made millions of dollars buying and selling businesses. He thought he knew everything. But he knew nothing about this new industry. So I taught him the system. He refused to follow it. He thought he had a better way. He ended up quitting because he was not getting any results.

The problem was not the system. The problem was that he refused to be coachable and follow the system.

Make sure you remain a teachable member of your Inner Table. Listen to their guidance. A Rich Life comes from being a life-long learner. You can't be all you are capable of becoming without the wisdom and guidance of the people at your Inner Table.

A Great Example of the Benefit of an Inner Table

A key function of your Inner Table is to help you identify your self-sabotaging habits—habits that you might not even be aware of. These self-sabotaging tendencies will rob you of a Rich Life on the Fly. I call them "blind spots."

I recently heard a conference speaker say that blind spots are "something someone believes they do well, but everyone on their team knows they do not." The goal of your Inner Table is to create a safe place where you can learn about your blind spots. For those of you who think you already know all your blind spots...you don't. And be aware: once you discover these blind spots, new ones always pop up.

I once led a Think Tank where I taught about blind spots. The participants strategized about the best ways to discover theirs and how to address them. One member, Sue, was a very well-liked woman who ran a successful business with over 25 employees. During our Think Tank, Sue said to the group, "What if you already know what your employees will tell you about your blind spots? What if you already know that you work too much, but you don't want to change?"

Sue assumed she knew her blind spot. She thought she had clarity on other people's perspectives on her. But what Sue didn't realize is that her staff did not think working too much was her blind spot. Instead, they felt micromanaged and under-appreciated.

This is why these character traits or habits are called blind spots: We can't see them on our own!

Using Your Inner Table to Improve Your Weaknesses

There are certain instances where, in order to be exceptional, we must confront our weaknesses and improve upon them. Most of the time, I want you to focus on developing your strengths (more on that in Step Three) and staffing your weaknesses. In other words, I want you to concentrate on what you do well and delegate or outsource what you don't.

Sometimes, though, we just can't staff a weakness. We have to suck it up and get good.

Sometimes, though, we just can't staff a weakness. We have to suck it up and get good.

I once worked with a very successful businessman named Steve whose position required him to have significant interaction with people. Steve loved to talk and tell stories. Storytelling was part of his charm. His clients loved him, but he eventually hit a plateau in his business. He was losing staff right and left, and his clients had leveled off.

Steve was smart enough to know he needed help. And what I learned as his executive coach is that Steve was so focused on connecting with people and telling stories that he stopped listening. As you'll see in Step Four, listening is critical to living a Rich Life. But Steve wasn't a good listener. His staff felt ignored and devalued, so they left. Steve had a glaring blind spot.

No matter how weak Steve was at listening, he could not delegate it. His business was dependent on communication for success. Through our coaching sessions, Steve learned how to listen effectively to others. More importantly, he discovered the success that comes from learning to grow in an area of weakness. I'm pleased to say that Steve had his best year last year bringing home seven figures. His staff now adores him and feels privileged to work for and learn from him.

Your Inner Table can help you achieve this sort of personal success, too. This is the place where you can be vulnerable. It's where you can strategize about how to handle your blind spots. It's your safe place to be real and still be held accountable.

Assemble Your Inner Table Before You Choose Your Path

Some of you might be reading this and thinking that it's premature for you to select and assemble your Inner Table. Maybe you're thinking, "First, I need to figure out which direction I should go." Or, "I need to do some research before I can put my Inner Table together." Stop that over-thinking! It will not serve you. It will actually hinder you from a Rich Life on the Fly. Instead, assemble your Inner Table *before* you decide your direction.

I have worked with many clients who have a tendency toward paralysis by over-analysis. They want to have all the details planned out before they bring anyone else in to help them. Your Inner Table will fill this wisdom gap. It's the bridge from where you are to where you should be and can be!

Don't make the mistake of going any farther in your journey without them. Assemble your Inner Table now. The sooner you do, the richer your life will become.

Your Inner Table Determines Your Future

> The people you spend time with matter. Show me your relationships and I'll show you your destiny.

The people you spend time with matter. Show me your relationships and I'll show you your destiny. If you get the people right, you get your life right. But quality relationships don't just happen without any forethought. You have to take the time to carefully and thoughtfully select who you want to be part of your A-Team. Assemble an Inner Table that will coach you, counsel you and support you.

As you start to assemble your Inner Table, ask yourself:

- Who has been where you want to go?
- Who challenges you to be better?
- Who is trustworthy and loyal?
- Who will hold you accountable?

At our workshops, we teach you exactly who in your life should take a seat at your Inner Table. You'll leave with a clear plan of how to invite each person with an offer they can't say "no" to. You'll discover the qualities that your members must have to guide you and fuel you to your dreams. We even map out a game plan to for inviting, assembling and leading your Inner Table discussions to build the life you are looking for.

Together, we'll identify your A-Team—the people who can fast-track you to your Rich Life on the Fly.

STEP TWO:
BUILD YOUR INNER TABLE
ACTION QUESTIONS

"For the things we have to learn before we can do them, we learn by doing them."

— Aristotle

1. What would your ideal Inner Table look like?

_____

_____

_____

_____

_____

2. What questions would you like to ask your Inner Table members?

_____

_____

_____

_____

_____

3. What kind of format or process do you plan to use to conduct productive Inner Table meetings?

_____

_____

_____

_____

_____

4. Who are some people you could approach to take a seat at your Inner Table?

_____

_____

_____

_____

_____

5. What current problems would you want solved at your Inner Table?

_____

_____

_____

_____

_____

6. How could you use your Inner Table to learn how to delegate your weaknesses?

_____

_____

_____

_____

_____

7. How could you add value to your Inner Table?

_____

_____

_____

_____

_____

STEP THREE:
LEVERAGE YOUR STRENGTHS

We each have unique gifts and talents. But what most people never learn is how to monetize their strengths. Learning this key strategy will help you to increase your income, build your wealth, develop your business and increase your sales. And, even better, you'll learn to work more efficiently so you have more time to enjoy the things you love!

Discover Your Strengths

You have unique gifts and talents. Part of the fun of life is discovering them. It's what sets you apart and gives you an advantage in life. You likely already have a pretty good idea of what your strengths are. However, if you are like most people, you are not using your strengths to their full potential.

Are You On the Right Path?

During my time as a trial lawyer, I thought I was operating in my strength zone. And in many ways, I was indeed playing to my strengths. I can think on my feet. I love engaging with an audience to build their self-awareness and broaden their perspective. In high school, I won state debate championships. In college, I directed the university's speakers' bureau. During law school, I won virtually every moot court and trial advocacy competition there was. Working in the trial department at a top international law firm in Chicago seemed like the perfect fit for me.

But it wasn't.

In a firm that size, most litigation was settled. It was rare that a case went to trial. Thus, I spent most of my days researching and writing. I spent very little time speaking, arguing and debating. My greatest strengths lay dormant. That was a tough reality to face. And it confirmed for me that I was not at all aligned with my strengths.

Are you on the right path? What are your strengths? Does the path you are on use your strengths? Does it allow you to develop those strengths? Is there a way you can make a shift to begin using them more? If you can't use them to their full potential in your career, can you use them to serve others outside of your work? Are you blessing others with your strengths? Do you find joy in what you are doing?

If not, it might be time to consider taking a new path.

Living a Rich Life on the Fly will depend on you using your gift: both to serve others and to generate income.

Finding Your Sweet Spot

In our workshops, we devote much time and attention to helping people discover their strengths and work in their "strength zone." However, on your own, you can begin to brainstorm and ask yourself the following questions:

- What do you do better than others?
- What do you do that elicits compliments about how well you do it?
- What do you do that comes easy to you but others think is challenging?

Try asking the five people closest to you what you do better than most anyone they know. In fact, ask your Inner

Table! You'll gain great insight on discovering your gift. I know you have one, because everyone does! Maybe it's something you do that just seems natural. You may not even be aware of it because you do it on autopilot. Maybe you can't even explain how you do it: you just know that it comes easy.

Your strength is something you want to make sure you are using. It will give you the greatest return on investment and the most success with the least amount of effort. Identify yours and focus on using it to serve others in your work place, family and community.

What is Your Income-Producing Gift?

Now that you have some insight on your strength, it's time to figure out how you can use it to build your wealth. We all have passions and gifts, but they are not always income-producing. The difference is important. For example, you may be passionate about gardening, but it isn't likely to earn you an income. You do, however, have a unique income-producing gift. Think for a moment: What gift do you have that can be monetized? What do you do better than most people and how can you use that skill or talent to increase your revenue? What skill do you possess that, when you are using it, people remark how exceptional you are? It's time to learn to make those strengths work for you.

My husband is one of those people whom everyone loves to be around. He's funny and charismatic and is an exceptional listener. Wherever he goes, people end up wanting to help him. It's crazy how people he's just met want to bend over backwards to help him become more successful! He's what I call a "connector."

Once he learned to monetize this gift, it became an income-producing gift for him. He is in several networking organizations and a men's tennis club, and he is involved with several groups and committees within our church. He begins by getting to know people. He listens. He makes them laugh. And he looks for a way to serve them. It's natural for him. And this is an income-producing gift because these contacts always end up referring him business, building his network and passing along opportunities.

We recently discovered that Brian was only spending about 30% of his time engaging in the activities that allowed him to connect with people. We sat down together and brainstormed some changes he could implement that would allow him to focus more time on his income-producing gift.

He started outsourcing projects, delegating more and even hiring a personal assistant. This freed him up to spend 80% of his time on his income-producing gift: connecting with people. He wasn't working any more hours than before: He was just working smarter. As a result, his sales are up 46% from this time last year! Can you imagine if you could earn 46% more just by making some subtle shifts in your behavior?

With the right planning and strategizing around your strengths, you can.

Stay in Your Strength Zone

In our events and workshops, we dig deeper to discover how you can transform your strength into your income-producing gift. You may already be aware of your strengths. But all too often, my clients know what they are good at, but they don't know how to monetize it. That's the secret sauce.

In our events, we show you how to work less and earn more by identifying your strengths and then putting them to use to make money for you. You want to spend as much time as you can in what I call your "strength zone." Aim to spend 80% of your working time on your income-producing gift, 10% developing it further and 10% problem-solving.

The key to this process is to delegate and outsource everything you can that does not involve your area of strength. Anything that is not furthering your goals and boosting your quality of life should be outsourced, delegated or ignored. At our workshops, I will give you the simple blue-print to put this into effect.

Determine the Hourly Rate of Your Work

The motto I have learned to live by is, "Work smarter, not harder." But that was not always second nature to me. As a lawyer, my day was all about billing hours. The longer a task takes, the more time a lawyer can bill to it. Most corporate lawyers are rewarded, promoted and bonused based on their billable hours. It's how productivity is measured. Sadly, the system often encourages the opposite of efficiency. But there is a golden nugget in how lawyers bill their time.

If you are not a lawyer, you may not have ever had the "joyful pleasure" of tracking your day in 15 minute increments. Although tedious, it's actually a very useful tool. I have seen huge revelations from asking my clients to track their time in 15 minute increments for a week.

I offer a free, downloadable time-tracker tool on my website. You will also find it in the back of this book. Use this tool for a full 5-day work week. Note the task or activity you are performing during each 15 minute increment of the day. If you are doing the same task for an hour, just draw a line down through that time period under the description.

The insight you will gain by tracking your time this way is truly remarkable. It will force you to turn off your "auto-pilot" mode and turn on some deep focus into your daily activities.

The next step is to analyze your time tracker. This is where we really dig in during our workshops so that we can teach you to shave hours off your week. In fact, my clients report that this exercise has helped them to boost their productivity while still decreasing their work time!

After you have tracked a particular day, assign a dollar amount to that task. Was it $20/hour, $100/hour or $1,000/hour work?

Twenty-dollar-an-hour work is work that someone else can probably do. The rule of thumb to keep in mind is that if someone else can perform the task 80% as well as you can, it's time to turn it over to someone else. In our live events, we show you how to outsource tasks even if you do not have staff or an assistant.

Hundred-dollar-an-hour work is more meaningful, but if you can train the right person to do it, it too can be delegated. In our workshops we will teach you some great delegation strategies to equip that person to get the result you want so you can really let go of that project or activity.

Thousand-dollar-an-hour work is work that only _____ (insert your full name) can do. These are your high impact, bottom line, income-producing activities. This is where you need to focus your time. This is your strength zone. This is where you truly use your income-producing gift. When you really master this, your thousand-dollar-an-hour work can actually become ten-thousand-dollar-an-hour work if you are truly in your strength zone.

Many of you will get the gist of the 15 minute tracker but you won't actually do it. Don't fall into that category of people. It's like having all the tools and materials at your fingertips but never actually building the dream house with it. You have to develop the self-awareness and focus that comes from actually using these tools. I guarantee that you will discover things you did not realize were sucking your time. And you'll realize how much of your day was spent on those time-sucking tasks.

It all boils down to focus. Focus is the key to wealth. You must focus the majority of your time on (1) using your strength to increase your income and (2) doing work that only you can do. Both Bill Gates and Warren Buffet were once asked, independently of one another, what had been the single most important factor in their success throughout their lives. They both gave the same single-word answer: Focus.

Focusing on doing what you do best will take you where you want to go.

Staffing Your Weaknesses

I have a client, Tami, who was once struggling with all the tasks she had to tackle to run her Internet business. When I met her, she was looking for solutions. She did not have an assistant to delegate any of her tasks to. Her efficiency was also some of the worst I have ever seen. Her days were filled with interruptions by seemingly urgent things that did nothing to build her business or increase her revenue. Tami was extremely hard-working and persistent. I have a lot of respect for her. She knew her business could be successful, and she knew she needed help finding a way to free up her time to focus on important, business-building, income-producing activities.

After attending several of my events and joining one of my Think Tanks, Tami got to the point where she had a system that allowed her to prioritize and stay focused on activities that furthered her business goals. We identified her income-producing gift. I taught her to hire a competent virtual assistant to handle tasks that she did not need to be doing. And then Tami, a single mom with a flat-lined Internet business, went on to grow her business and achieve incredible financial and professional success.

Tami learned one of the secrets of a Rich Life on the Fly. She discovered the art of delegating tasks that did not involve her income-producing gift. She learned how to out-source her weaknesses. No longer drowning in busy-ness, she could focus on activities that involved business-building strengths.

Where do your personal weaknesses creep into your daily tasks or activities? Maybe it's something you just aren't as good at or do not like doing. Maybe it's simply something you continually put off doing. Maybe a past failure makes you avoid tasks involving that weakness at all costs.

Whatever the case, use your Inner Table to help you to determine:

- Which weaknesses you can, in fact, delegate
- To whom you can delegate these tasks
- A deadline for following through with this delegation
- A plan to follow up on and re-evaluate these decisions

Like Tami, once you staff your weaknesses, you'll find that you can focus more on building not only your professional life but also the personal life of your dreams.

It's all about discovering how to transfer your strength into an income-producing gift and delegate work involving your weaknesses. This is when your efficiency will really soar. Your income will increase and you'll have newfound time to focus on the things important to you. You'll find that you can focus more on building a quality Rich Life. You'll find that you can really begin to Live on the Fly.

> We can't give our best in our work without making time to recharge and refill our tanks.

Family Time and YOU Time is Thousand-Dollar-an-Hour Work

One of the greatest gifts I've received is the joy of helping an overworked, overstressed entrepreneur discover the formula for earning more and working less so they can find time for themselves and their family. You see, we can't give our best in our work without making time to recharge and refill our tanks.

As I've said, a Rich Life is not just about money: It's also about the quality of our relationships and our lives. By becoming supernaturally efficient and working in your strength zone, you will gain back valuable hours that you can devote to living a quality life.

Now, here's where you should pay special attention: It is critical that you do not spend this newly free time on income-producing activities. To live a regret-free, Rich Life, you must focus on your quality of life outside of work.

During the time I was a workaholic, I don't think I was even conscious of the order of my priorities. I loved my family very much. But the decisions I was making and the way I was working did not reflect my values: I wasn't prioritizing my family.

Maybe you can relate to this story. One afternoon, many years ago, I decided to surprise our two-year-old daughter and come home from work a little early to enjoy the afternoon with her. I did not even let Sulma, our nanny, know I was coming home early.

I imagined that I would open the front door, announce I was home and see my daughter running toward me and squealing with excitement. Instead, I found her in her high chair. There was no excitement. No squealing. She just looked at me and then at her nanny and said, "No Mommy, you go…I don't want you, I want Sulma."

My heart sank. I was devastated. I was angry. I was embarrassed.

I decided then to make some significant changes to my priorities and my professional and personal life.

Maybe you've already faced a moment of guilt and regret like mine. But even if you haven't, I don't want you to wait for that moment to make changes in your own life. This is your chance to live a Rich Life filled with joy and happiness.

Don't wait for your Rich Life to happen to you. Make it happen. And make it happen now.

STEP THREE: LEVERAGE YOUR STRENGTHS ACTION QUESTIONS

"Tell me and I forget. Teach me and I remember. Involve me and I learn."

— Benjamin Franklin

1. Which of your daily activities involves your greatest strength?

   _____

   _____

   _____

   _____

2. What adjustments could you make to spend more time every day in your area of strength?

_____

_____

_____

_____

_____

3. How could you generate income, or more income, by using your gift?

_____

_____

_____

_____

_____

4. How could you further develop your strength to become exceptional at it?

_____

_____

_____

_____

_____

5. How can you market your strength to your clients, customers or patients in a way that distinguishes you?

   _____

   _____

   _____

   _____

   _____

6. What is your plan to intentionally grow your strength this year?

   _____

   _____

   _____

   _____

   _____

7. How can you bless others or give back using your strength?

   _____

   _____

   _____

   _____

   _____

STEP FOUR:
BECOME A WORLD CLASS COMMUNICATOR

This may be the chapter that I get most excited about. I love teaching people to become more effective communicators. Why? Because it's where they see the most immediate results in their sales, referrals and in the quality of their relationships.

Communicating to Connect

Being a great communicator is actually not about speaking at all. That seems strange, right? But it's true. The most effective communicators are the ones who listen the most and ask the best questions.

Have you ever been around someone who just makes you feel heard and who makes you feel better about yourself? Isn't that the kind of person you want to be? One who encourages, lifts and learns about people? It's the kind of communicator you must be to live a Rich Life on the Fly.

I wasn't always an effective communicator. I used to think that being a good communicator meant being able to articulate my ideas well or tell a story people could laugh at or relate to. Maybe you're thinking, "That's what I thought, too…you mean it's not?" The truth is that we can connect by speaking, but ultimately the most effective way to connect is by listening.

The late Malcolm Forbes, the entrepreneur and publisher of Forbes magazine, once said, "The art of conversation lies in listening." Great listening is the key to all effective communication.

But most people listen only in order to respond. And a lot of people listen to interrupt. You're probably thinking of someone right now who never lets you finish your sentence. They have always done something bigger and better. These "one-uppers" are often not even aware of their terrible listening skills. They think they are relating to you and sharing a similar experience. They think their story must be told. They often respond with, "Oh you think that's bad, listen to what happened to me."

You never want to be a "one-upper!" Instead, you want to be an effective communicator. And that means that you must be an effective listener.

Be an Empathetic Listener

A truly great communicator listens to understand. Have you ever listened to someone in order to imagine what it would feel like to be them? Have you ever tried to listen while trying on the other person's point of view, their life experiences and their perspective? The exercise requires putting your experiences and your autobiography aside. It takes effort for most of us. It's an art. And learning it will change your life.

In fact, numerous studies link empathy to better business results. When someone is truly heard, they are far more likely to hear you and see your perspective. Moreover, they are far more likely to perform better as a result of being understood. Better yet, empathy reduces racism, prejudice and bullying. It boosts creativity and improves relationships. And it's actually a very simple thing to do. Just listen fully and completely to the other person. Ask questions. Imagine what it's like to be them. And then practice these skills over and over again.

So focus on the next conversation you have today. Are you listening to respond, or are you listening to feel what it's really like to be in that person's shoes? As you pay more attention to building your empathetic listening skills, you will begin to cross over into great communicator land. You will begin to attract more clients, more referrals and more sales.

By building empathy, you will also build a Rich Life on the Fly.

Good Listening is Hard Work

Have you ever found yourself listening to someone thinking, "Will you just get to the point?" Have you ever listened to someone knowing exactly what you will say as soon as there is a brief pause in the conversation?

These kinds of listening habits can hurt your relationships and hinder your success. And they can hold you back from the momentum you could be experiencing in your business.

When I was a trial lawyer, my clients were paying top dollar for my advice and strategy. I thought I was supposed to talk more than listen because that is what they wanted from me. The truth is that even experts who get paid for their advice are far more effective when they listen and ask great questions. Listening allows you to discern what the other person really wants instead of assuming what you think they want. This distinction will take you from an average business person to a world class one.

But listening is often a struggle for busy entrepreneurs and professionals. We are trained to have solutions, provide answers and give advice. We are busy. We need others to talk fast and get to the point. And when they don't, we tend to assist them. Our busy lives lead us to listen in order to respond, to interrupt or to judge.

> When we fail to listen with discernment and empathy, we prevent ourselves from leaving a lasting impression on others. We stand in the way of our own potential.

But that's not what it means to truly listen to someone. When we fail to listen with discernment and empathy, we prevent ourselves from leaving a lasting impression on others. We stand in the way of our own potential.

The good news is that we can change those bad habits.

Now that you know that great communicating is really more about how you listen than it is about what you say, let's talk about the benefits.

Benefits of Great Listening:

- Better leadership
- More sales and referrals
- Increased staff and customer loyalty
- Faster promotion
- Better relationships
- Reduced conflict
- Increased happiness
- Improved perception of personal intelligence

Shut Up and Listen

Isn't it interesting that we are taught how to read, write and speak but not how to listen? As a result, poor listening is more common than poor speaking. Yet listening is the most important skill of all when it comes to the success that lies ahead.

The secret, I've learned, is in knowing when to be silent and just listen. It takes self-control and self-awareness. Some people are naturally better at it. Others have to work harder to master it. And still others think they are good at it but are sorely mistaken.

As a former debate champion, trial lawyer and public speaker, I used to struggle with the idea of active, empathetic listening. It ran contrary to everything I believed. And I had to literally lose my voice before I could really see the benefits of listening.

It happened recently at a large conference devoted to women's professional development. I was one of the speakers. Thankfully, I was able to give my talk—but just after, I began to lose my voice. I was forced to go through the day in "listen only" mode. Thus, I spent most of my subsequent networking time just listening. And you know what? I found that I became far more observant of others: the words they spoke, their tone of voice, their emotion and passion behind their ideas. I also found that I achieved some surprising success. After I returned home from the event, I received numerous e-mails about how much everyone enjoyed me and learned from me. I had barely even spoken to them: I mostly listened! And yet after this conference, I had the highest percentage of people ever who registered for my webinar course after an event. Many of them even referred other friends to me.

What I learned was this: Listening is the greatest way to show someone respect. Far more is gained by surrendering the floor than by dominating it. The second a person senses that they are being understood and listened to, they become more motivated to see your point of view, buy what you are selling or recommend and refer to you.

It's amazing what can happen when you listen.

How Our Time is Spent Communicating: The Grim Reality

Our Time Spent Communicating*

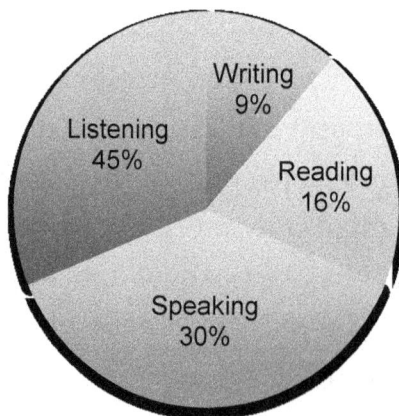

* Lee, Dick & Delmar Hatesohl, *Listening: Our Most Used Communication Skill*, Retrieved from http://extension.missouri.edu/p/CM150

We spend roughly 70 to 80% of our lives communicating. This is how we spend that that time:

We spend on average 9% writing, 16% reading, 30% speaking and 45% listening.

However, we only comprehend about 25% of what we hear. We're spending nearly half of our communicating time listening, but we're not understanding most of what we hear. The world is not listening! But *you* can start listening well. This is your golden opportunity to be set apart from the masses!

Two Exercises to Become a Better Listener

One of the best ways to improve your listening skills is to spend time in silence. Even just three minutes a day of silence helps. Use this time to practice really hearing all the sounds around you.

I like to do my three minutes while I am in the car. With four kids, silence really is golden when I am driving alone! I listen to each car passing by, the rattling of my water bottle, the air conditioning, my car accelerating or decelerating, a plane flying overhead. Try the same in your own car, or somewhere else where you can fully focus your attention. By doing this, we train ourselves not just to hear, but to actively listen.

Another proven strategy to enhance your level of listening is to begin to notice all the different channels of sounds around you. For example, the next time you are grabbing coffee, stop to listen to the sounds of the various conversations around you. Focus on one at a time. Listen for the sound of the coffee brewing in the background, the cash register opening or the door opening and closing as someone enters or exits the cafe. Train your brain to really hear and register each and every sound from all these various channels.

You can also do this listening exercise outside in nature: in the woods, at a lake or by the ocean. Conscious listening creates understanding. Understanding creates connection. And when you habitually connect with others, you can maximize life's opportunities.

Fives Ways to Improve Your Listening

Active listening will change your relationships and make you a far more effective communicator. So how can you develop or improve your listening skills to become a world class communicator? Try these techniques on your spouse, your family, your coworkers and your clients.

1. <u>Be Quiet and Listen</u> — Stop talking! Listen for what the other person is feeling and what they need. The act of simply being silent and repeating the other side's position or argument before you begin to talk has been found to enhance conflict resolution by as much as 50%.

2. <u>Suspend Judgment</u> — Often our empathy is hindered by judgment or our own experiences. Stop and take time to get to know the cashier at the grocery store, or that tattooed waitress with piercings. Your world view likely projects a stereotype that is completely off base. Attempt to have a conversation at least once or twice a week where you try to get to know someone you may otherwise dismiss or judge. This simple behavior will rewire you to be more empathetic.

3. <u>Look Them in the Eye</u> — Try looking someone so deeply in the eye that you can actually articulate the emotions you believe they are feeling. Studies show that this practice can enhance your compassion and empathy.

4. <u>Teach Empathy</u> — The best way to learn is to teach. Begin to teach your co-workers, spouse, children, team and friends about empathy. Talk about asking questions such as: "What are they thinking?" "What is he feeling?"

5. <u>Invite More Information</u> — Ask open-ended questions. Allow your questions to come from a place of genuine interest and curiosity. Your interest in the other person should convey that they are the most important thing in your world right at that moment.

Get Curious and Boost Your Sales

I told you that my husband is one of the best listeners I know. As a result, he is also one of the best sales people I know. And I've learned so much from him just by listening to him take incoming sales calls.

Initially there is complete silence. For minutes, I wonder how in the world he will land this deal when he doesn't even speak! When I asked him about this, he said, "You have to let them talk, and they will give you all the information you need to close the deal."

He gives the other person the space to talk and then waits for them to stop or to pause before asking an open-ended question that will get them talking more: questions as simple as, "Tell me: what are you looking for?" He said, "Once you understand that the sale is not about you, you can be so much more effective."

Listen

Ask a question to discover more about their needs.

Use that information to offer them exactly what they want and need!

Brian's goal is to listen long enough to completely understand their needs and to learn how he can best serve them. Sometimes this means listening to people ramble or go off on personal tangents. (Remember to set expectations about how much time you can devote to the call at the beginning of your own conversations!) These are the moments where he can really connect with the person on the other end of the conversation. And I have observed firsthand how this behavior results in people wanting to help my husband, teach him and refer business to him.

What does he do that's so special? It's something that *you* can do, too. He finds common ground with others. He uses humor. And he remains curious about the other person. In fact, becoming curious is a core foundation for being an effective communicator. It allows us to be empathetic and compassionate. And the best way to become curious is to slow down. Stop rushing conversations and start enjoying them. Allow the speaker to finish without interrupting or finishing their thought for them. Instead of judging or responding, begin to wonder. Ask, "I wonder why they would say that?"

Over the next 24 hours, pay attention to how much of your day you spend talking versus listening. Be genuinely interested in others. Notice if you have a tendency to interrupt or rush a conversation or plan your response while someone else is still speaking.

In our workshops, we notch your listening up another level. You will learn how to relate to every personality type. You'll discover what motivates each type of person, how to talk to them, how to sell to them and how to speak their language. Even the most difficult people. It's a life-changing lesson. Until then, practice listening to understand. As Sir Richard Branson said, "Listen more than you talk. Nobody ever learned anything by hearing themselves speak."

A Rich Life on the Fly Living Without Regrets

As people near the end of their lives, few, if any, ever say, "I wish I would have worked harder." They don't say, "I wish I would have stayed at the office longer so I could have gotten that promotion faster." They don't say, "I wish I would have driven a nicer car."

Instead, they often have deeper, more personal regrets. Regrets about not spending enough time with their families. Regrets about not cultivating more meaningful friendships. Regrets about unkind words, or unspoken love.

Living a Rich Life on the Fly is about living without regrets. It's investing in relationships and happiness. It's making adjustments to your life so that you are proud of who you are and of the life you are living. It's making time for your family, your friends, your health and your hobbies. That's a Rich Life on the Fly!

STEP FOUR:
BECOME A WORLD CLASS COMMUNICATOR
ACTION QUESTIONS

"The way to get started is to quit talking and begin doing."
— Walt Disney

1. On a scale of 1 to 10, how would you rate yourself as a listener?

   _____

2. Can you think of one or two people in your life who exemplify excellent listening?

   _____

   _____

3. What is it they do that makes them such effective communicators?

   _____

   _____

   _____

   _____

   _____

   _____

4. How can you learn from and model their level of listening?

_____

_____

_____

_____

_____

5. What would it look like to listen to someone and literally feel what it is like to walk in their shoes?

_____

_____

_____

_____

_____

6. Stop what you're doing right now, and listen to the sounds or silence all around you. How do you feel when you are fully listening without intending to respond?

_____

_____

_____

_____

_____

7. Whom can you teach about empathetic listening, and what will you tell them?

_____

_____

_____

_____

_____

_____

_____

_____

STEP FIVE:
FOLLOW THE CLUES

Experience is a great teacher, especially when it's someone else's. My dad used to always tell me, "Dawn, learn from someone else's mistakes so you don't have to make your own." I've made my fair share of my own mistakes. I'm sure you have, too. But there is incredible wisdom to be gained in learning from others' mistakes.

Success Leaves Clues

A life philosophy I live by is to study and model other successful people. You can learn so much from the successes, failures and behaviors of others! Whenever I begin a new endeavor, I find the very best person I can in that area of expertise, and I study them. I learn everything I can from them. If I can meet with them personally, I do. If I can't, I watch and learn from them. This strategy has served me well. It will serve you, too. Let me show you what I mean.

Becoming a Real Estate Investor

At the end of my legal career, I knew I wanted to try something new. It was 2006, right when the economy was tanking. Foreclosures were beginning to abound. And I saw a huge opportunity: Perhaps, I thought, I could begin a new career in foreclosure investing. But I knew better than to attempt such a risky endeavor without studying and understanding it.

I found the person I believed was the foremost expert on foreclosure investing. I was living in South Florida and she happened to be located in Sacramento, California. I started by listening to all of her calls. I studied her website and purchased her CDs. Then, I flew out to Sacramento for a boot camp where I learned the art of foreclosure investing in any market. Eventually, I entered her pricey mentorship program.

It was a significant investment of my time and money. But you know what? It all paid off when I made over $85,000 flipping my first house. I used to joke that it was beginner's luck. But it wasn't. It was because I had studied and learned from the best. I sold a total of 11 homes in less than two years. Better yet, I earned a huge profit on each one. I was even featured in Money Magazine for my foreclosure investing.

You can achieve astronomical success, too. But few of us can do it alone. We need teachers, mentors and coaches. So ask yourself: Whom can you find to mentor you in an area that you want to learn about or study?

Don't Be Afraid to Ask

Think about someone who has been where you'd like to go: someone who has the kind of success, lifestyle or expertise you'd love to have.

Now think about what it would be like to have them as your mentor. It would be pretty great, right?

And yet the biggest mistake I see people make is assuming that their ideal mentor is probably too busy to help them. It reminds me of a great saying: "The best way to get something done is to ask the busiest person you know to do it." Busy, successful professionals tend to be very efficient. They also tend to want to help others who are aspiring for greatness. You just have to be ready to convince them why you are the one they should help.

Have the confidence to ask. What have you got to lose? If you don't know the person personally, be ready to make your pitch. Practice telling them why they should help you with your professional career. Why are you worth their time? What do you have to offer them? Make it short and to the point. Furthermore, do your research before you speak to them. What drives them? What are some of their biggest successes? Can you find any information about their failures? What are their professional and civic interests? Answering these questions can give you the fuel to be able to tell them exactly why you are seeking them as your mentor. It also demonstrates your character and work ethic.

If you are unable to reach someone personally, you don't need to write them off as a potential mentor. You can study them by reading their books, listening to podcasts, attending their events and modeling their behavior.

Finally, don't stop at one mentor. Look at various people who can help you in different aspects of your career. Take a look around you right now at some of the experts and leaders in your community. Ask a lot of great questions. Practice your active listening. The nuggets you can take away are gold!

Becoming a Leadership Expert

I have always been fascinated by leadership. I remember being in high school and trying to mimic the style and behavior of great leaders. This practice served me well. Even back then, I was on to a key step to a Rich Life.

Success leaves clues. All we have to do is follow them.

Years ago, I discovered a man I believe to be the number one leadership expert in the world: John Maxwell. I began to study him intensely. John has authored and published over 75 books on leadership—many of them New York Times bestsellers. He speaks to Fortune 500 companies, presidents of nations and many of the world's top business executives. The more I learned about him, the more I realized that I had to learn what he knew! I read his books, listened to everything I could find and attended any live event I could get to.

> # Success leaves clues. All we have to do is follow them.

Back in 2011, I received a video invitation to join the John Maxwell Team as a Certified John Maxwell coach. I had the opportunity to study under John—not just to read his books and listen to his CDs but to truly work with him. And it was one of the best things I have ever done. But this opportunity only became available to me when it did because I had been following John so closely.

I had followed the clues of his success. And it enabled me to achieve that success, too.

You can do the same in your own life. Don't just wish for success: really research, learn and mimic others' success. Make the habits of success a part of your own life and routines.

In our workshops, you'll learn more about how to follow the clues of success. Whatever your dreams and aspirations are, these clues are out there!

Becoming a Direct Sales Leader

I want to give you one more example of how I studied someone who had been where I wanted to go. When I was first introduced to the world of direct sales, I loved the concept of residual income. I still do. I began in a simple start-up company that offered members the ability to shop online from over 3,000 of the top retailers. We all got cash back and built teams where we taught them to do the same thing. It was a brilliant business model at the right time. Internet shopping was catching on, and people were recognizing the convenience of it.

This particular Internet company ended up going under, but it taught me the basics of the industry. And I made six figures figuring it out on my own. Then the thought occurred to me: imagine what I could do if I had a mentor!

I then discovered a company with a 20-year track record—a company I knew would not go under like the previous one. Then, I found the person I believed to be the most experienced, most successful person in that company. She happened to live in Baltimore. After many phone conversations, I joined her team. I flew out to learn from her. I started putting into practice the things she taught me. My team began to grow. I found momentum. Then, she started coming to Florida at least once a month to coach me and help me build my team.

Less than a year later, my business partner and I had hit the position of Regional Vice President, the second highest position in this international company. We had set a record and had built an international team.

I couldn't have done this without the guidance of the person who mentored me.

It's amazing what happens when you learn from an expert. Who do you know who is an expert in your field? How can you begin to learn from them today?

What Do You Really Want to Be Exceptional At?

Regardless of what your passion or interests are, you can become an expert simply by seeking out other experts. If possible, try to find someone in your area and invite them to coffee. You'd be surprised who will accept your offer. Most successful people have been mentored and coached, and they thoroughly enjoy passing on what they know.

If you are not able to meet in person with the expert you are following, study them. Read everything they write, subscribe to all their social media channels, order their CDs and attend their events. You can learn so much from just observing them in action.

Ask the following questions as you study them:

- What is their system?
- What is their approach?
- How do they build their audience or client base?
- How do they spend their time?
- What do they do to get better?
- With whom are they surrounding themselves?
- What are their values?

- How do they spend their free time?

- What is their work/life balance?

- Who is on their team?

- How do they sell?

- What is their irresistible offer and how do they capitalize on it?

These were all questions I asked myself as I studied John Maxwell. I could glean the answers to almost every question just by observing him. For example, I read that every year during the week between Christmas and New Year's, he reflects on his year's work. He does not make any appointments or meetings that week. He just reviews his entire calendar for the past year by asking:

- What did I do well that I should repeat?

- What was a mistake that I should not repeat?

- Where could I be more efficient?

- How can I get better?

Ever since I read that, I have spent the week between Christmas and New Year's reflecting on my own calendar and asking these questions. It has made me a better leader and a more efficient and successful business woman, mother and wife.

So find someone—or a few someones—to be your mentor. One day, you just might become a sought-out mentor for someone else, too.

STEP FIVE:
FOLLOW THE CLUES
ACTION QUESTIONS

"I am always doing that which I cannot do, in order that I may learn how to do it."

— Pablo Picasso

1. Who would you like to be your potential mentor?

    _____

    _____

2. What do they do that makes them an appealing mentor?

    _____

    _____

    _____

    _____

    _____

3. What would you ask this mentor if you had an hour with them?

_____

_____

_____

_____

_____

4. How do you think they problem-solve?

_____

_____

_____

_____

_____

5. What is their irresistible offer?

_____

_____

_____

_____

_____

6. How can you implement some of these "clues" into your life?

_____

_____

_____

_____

_____

_____

7. One of the best ways to grow is to find great learning resources. What two books could you read to help you model the habits and practices of your potential mentor(s)?

_____

_____

YOUR RICH LIFE

I am passionate and extremely excited to help you increase your income, build your business and develop the life you have dreamed of! I want to see you live a Rich Life on the Fly.

Take Action!

I hope this book serves as a pivotal point in your life. The greatest change comes from my clients who see an open door and rush through it. This is your door! Will you rush through it? Research shows us that our positive thoughts, good intentions and great ideas can actually transform us,

become habits and change the course of our lives—if we take action in the moment. The key is taking action now! Will you join me at a Think Tank? Come to a live event? Explore coaching? What will you do to live a Rich Life on the Fly?

> You sow what you reap. What you do, the decisions you make and the actions you take all come back to you. They determine the life you are living. The choices you make today determine the stories you will tell tomorrow.

No excuses. No fear. No regret. No doubt. No procrastination.

If I had not listened to God's voice to stay home with our kids, I would not have learned the formula for living a Rich Life on the Fly. If I had not begun to write out the five steps to a Rich Life, I wouldn't have been able to have a blueprint to take action. If I had not begun to act on my blueprint, I wouldn't be living the Rich Life on the Fly I am living today.

You sow what you reap. What you do, the decisions you make and the actions you take all come back to you. They determine the life you are living. The choices you make today determine the stories you will tell tomorrow.

Will you let this book sit on your computer, tablet or shelf? Or will you let it change your life? I'm proof that it can. The clients who I coach and who are in my Think Tanks and come to my events are all proof that it can!

The Time is NOW

Life is good when your relationships are good. Life is great when your relationships are good and your business is thriving. What steps can you take *today* to begin to live a Rich Life on the Fly?

You did not come across this book by accident or coincidence. Either you will make a decision right now to change your life with what you have learned, or you will go back to living a life that fills you with stress, fear, guilt and regret.

Unless you persevere to live the life you deserve, you'll live wondering what you were really capable of. Don't be the person who reaches the end of their life filled with regret. Don't wish you did it better and lived a fuller, more joyful life. Decide to start living it today!

I want you to be the next success story. Your influence, your legacy and the quality of your life has less to do with your title and position than it does with the life you are living. Make a decision to overcome all the excuses and obstacles and start creating a Rich Life. Start loving the life you have. Start making decisions to live the life you deserve!

Join Me!

Imagine joining me and other like-minded people who are ready to change their lives. Imagine what it would be like to embark on the journey to make lots of money and to enjoy all that it has to offer. Imagine having satisfying relationships, joy in your day and time for hobbies and for giving back. Imagine what it is like to earn significantly more money while working less. Imagine the time you could have to go on vacations with your friends and family. To give back. To discover new hobbies.

I want you to join me on an amazing adventure to your Rich Life on the Fly. Go to my website DawnConnelly.com and register now to join me at my next live event, webinar or Think Tank. I want to meet you. I want you to be connected with a culture that will change your life.

There is nothing like getting away from your day-to-day life and spending time with like-minded people learning to map out and live the life you dream of. Come get all the skills and the vision to take your career and your personal life exactly where you want it go.

Make the decision now to push ahead. To stop wasting time. To stop living in fear. To stop feeling stressed and overwhelmed. There is more! You have nothing to lose but everything to gain. Connect with me at DawnConnelly.com.

Get Started Today!

Growth doesn't just happen. You won't automatically get better without a plan. What's your plan? Without one, things will go back to the way they have always been as soon as you are done with this book. But that doesn't have to happen. I can teach you how to identify your income-producing gift and how to spend 80% of your working time in your strength zone. I can teach you to live the life you should be living.

Create your Rich Life. It requires your action. Your commitment.

So decide to decrease your stress. Build a quality life with your loved ones. Live a no-regret life full of happiness and joy. Please get started today! Let's begin this journey together!

About the Author

Dawn is an executive coach and keynote speaker who conducts Think Tanks and workshops for leaders, entrepreneurs, corporations, businesses and professionals. She also coaches and develops exciting live events for those who want to become the very best version of themselves.

Dawn loves teaching people the secret to a Rich Life. She teaches this formula in her workshops, live events and webinars.

Dawn is a certified and founding member of the John Maxwell Team. She has shared the stage with leadership expert John Maxwell and motivational speaker Nick Vujicic.

Dawn was a national trainer and advisory board member for several years for a direct sales company where she taught thousands of people leadership principles, such as how to become better communicators and how to harness their full potential. She became a Regional Vice President in another international direct sales company in under one year, setting a record for that company. In that time, Dawn gained insight and experience on the importance of team-building as she built world-wide teams.

Dawn graduated Phi Beta Kappa from the University of Florida and attended law school at Chicago-Kent College of Law. She clerked for the Honorable Blanche M. Manning of the U.S. District Court for the Northern District of Illinois. Dawn is licensed to practice law in Illinois and Florida.

Dawn practiced commercial litigation at an international law firm in their Chicago and Miami offices for nine years.

In her practice of law, Dawn received an award for Outstanding Achievement and Commitment to Pro Bono Service in the Community. Her most fulfilling moment as a lawyer was winning asylum for an Albanian woman who was sex-trafficked from Albania to Italy where she was raped, beaten and starved before escaping to Chicago. The case established Dawn's belief in servant leadership.

Dawn is married to her high school sweetheart, Brian. They live in Palm City, Florida, with their four children.

RICH LIFE 15 MINUTE TRACKER	Day and Date:

Time	Activity
6:00 AM	
6:15 AM	
6:30 AM	
6:45 AM	
7:00 AM	
7:15 AM	
7:30 AM	
7:45 AM	
8:00 AM	
8;15 AM	
8:30 AM	
8:45 AM	
9:00 AM	
9:15 AM	
9:30 AM	
9:45 AM	
10:00 AM	
10:15 AM	
10:30 AM	
10:45 AM	
11:00 AM	
11:15 AM	

Time	Activity
11:30 AM	
11:45 AM	
12:00 PM	
12:15 PM	
12:30 PM	
12:45 PM	
1:00 PM	
1:15 PM	
1:30 PM	
1:45 PM	
2:00 PM	
2:15 PM	
2:30 PM	
2:45 PM	
3:00 PM	
3:15 PM	
3:30 PM	
3:45 PM	
4:00 PM	
4:15 PM	
4:30 PM	
4:45 PM	
5:00 PM	
5:15 PM	

Time	Activity
5:30 PM	
5:45 PM	
6:00 PM	
6:15 PM	
6:30 PM	
6:45 PM	
7:00 PM	
7:15 PM	
7:30 PM	
7:45 PM	
8:00 PM	
8:15 PM	
8:30 PM	
8:45 PM	
9:00 PM	
9:15 PM	
9:30 PM	
9:45 PM	